I0470940

110% Success™

Insights and Quotes to Move You and Your Company Forward

David M. Shedd

Table of Contents

Table of Contents

Chapter 1: Introduction

"Your best is not good enough. You must give 110%."

Across sports fields, classrooms, factories, offices, and households, this cry will ring out countless thousands of times today. It is as if by sheer force of will, by total commitment, and by tremendous effort alone, we will accomplish our goals and achieve victory.

While hard work and consistent effort are important to achieving business, sports or personal success, they are over-emphasized. As we will see from this book, success (and happiness) comes from effort (yes), but also from doing the right, wise and good things and from being an intelligent, thoughtful and ethical person (or leader) today and every day.

"We should hunt out the helpful pieces of teaching, and the spirited and noble-minded sayings which are capable of immediate practical application and learn them so well that words become works."
Seneca (Ancient Roman Stoic philosopher)

"Everything has been said before, but since nobody listens we have to keep going back and begin all over again."
André Gide (20th century French writer)

This book contains 110 insights into business and personal success. Individually, none of them are surprising; they are all fundamental.

Each insight is backed up by one or several quotations from the collective wisdom of businesspeople, politicians, leaders and individuals. As will become abundantly clear, the fundamentals to success in politics, business, and life have been observed and recorded by wise individuals across continents and throughout history.

Collectively then, the insights and quotations are inspiring. They allow us to avoid starting from scratch. We can stand upon the shoulders of others, reflect upon their insights, learn from their wisdom, and propel ourselves and our companies to success.

This book will not move your company forward!

This book will not make you a better business leader!

This book will not help you fulfill your business and personal goals!

But, then again, no book can solve your company's problems, make you a better business leader, and help you fulfill your dreams.

Only you can do it!

The challenge in writing any book on success in business is that the problems and conditions that each businessperson faces are unique. The strengths and weaknesses of each person's company, the marketplace, and the competition are unique. Each person's personality along with her likes and dislikes and strengths and weaknesses are unique. Each team is unique.

To be successful (both in business and personally) in such a unique situation requires that each person figure out a solution that works for his situation, personality, and company's culture.

As such, this book and the insights within need to be used as suggestions, reminders, and guideposts to help you discover the way forward for you and your company.

Best wishes and best of luck in realizing your success!

Chapter 2: A Successful Company Has a Good Leader

Section I: Why Leadership?

1. For the success of your company, good leadership is vital

"Everything rises and falls on leadership." John Maxwell (Leadership consultant)

"Men make history and not the other way around. In periods where there is no leadership, society stands still. Progress occurs when courageous, skilled leaders seize the opportunity to change things for the better." Harry S. Truman (33rd President of the United States)

"Most companies fail because of managerial error, but not many senior executives involved will admit that fact." Roger Connors et al (Authors of The Oz Principle)

"The Organizational Behavior class at Harvard Business School turns out to be the most important class you can take. Because your ability to attract people, to pay them the right way, to create culture and values and reinforce them, that's makes companies great." Jeffrey Immelt (CEO of GE)

Section II: What Makes a Leader?

2. A leader unites other individuals and propels them to a common success

"A leader is an individual who can consistently cause others to win." Unknown

"Leadership is creating an environment in which people want to be part of the organization and not just work for the organization." Horst Schulze (CEO of Ritz-Carlton)

"Leadership focuses on people. My definition of a leader is someone who helps people succeed." Carol Bartz (Former CEO of Autodesk and Yahoo!)

"You can't be a good leader unless you generally like people. That is how you bring out the best in them." Richard Branson (CEO of Virgin)

"Leadership is communicating to people their worth and potential so clearly that they come to see it in themselves." Stephen Covey (Author of <u>The Seven Habits of Highly Effective People</u>)

3. A leader has and attracts followers

"A leader is not a leader by rank, or title, or lineage. A leader is a leader because people are willing to follow. If a leader looks behind and nobody is following, he is not a leader – he is just out for a walk." Joseph Paris (18th century banker)

"As a leader, you get the people you deserve. Great people want to work for great leaders." Brad Sugars (Australian business coach)

"If your actions create a legacy that inspires others to dream more, learn more, do more, and become more, then you are an excellent leader." Dolly Parton (Country music star)

Section III: Good Leadership is Ethical Leadership

4. An ethical leader has integrity and character

"The supreme quality of leadership is unquestionably integrity. Without it, no real success is possible no matter whether it is on a section gang, a football field, in an army, or in an office." Dwight D. Eisenhower (34th President of the United States)

"Principled leaders make a difference in the world. To be a principled leader, a person must have many skills and qualities, including the highest standards of integrity, sound judgment, and a strong moral compass – an intuitive sense of what is right and wrong." Kim Clark (Former Dean of Harvard Business School)

"The lesson I learned from this is that it's easier to hold to your principles 100% of the time than it is to hold to them 98% of the time. If you give in to "just this once," based on a marginal cost analysis, as some of my former classmates have done, you'll regret where you end up. You've got to define for yourself what you stand for and draw the line in a safe place." Clayton Christensen (Harvard Business School Professor)

"The secret of life is honesty and fair dealing. If you can fake that, you've got it made." Groucho Marx (20th century American Comedian)

5. An ethical leader engenders trust

"Trust is the essence of leadership." Colin Powell (US General and former Secretary of State)

JP Morgan was being testified in Congress by Samuel Untermeyer, a relentless corporate lawyer. Untermeyer asked Morgan if the main criterion for lending was the money or property of the borrower. "No, sir," Morgan said. "The first thing is character." "Before money or property?" Untermeyer asked. "Before money or property or anything else," Morgan said. "A man I do not trust could not get money from me on all the bonds in Christendom." JP Morgan (19th century American banker)

6. An ethical leader leads by his or her own immaculate example

"The time is always right to do what is right." Martin Luther King, Jr. (American Civil Rights leader)

"Example is not the main thing in influencing others. It is the only thing. Example is leadership." Albert Schweitzer (Early 20th century German theologian, scientist and humanist)

"What you do speaks so loudly that I can't hear what you say." Ralph Waldo Emerson (19th century American poet)

"Sir, are you so grossly ignorant of human nature as not to know that a man may be very sincere in good principles without having good practice?" Dr. Samuel Johnson (18th century English author)

"Do the right thing. It will gratify some people and astonish the rest." Mark Twain (19th century American author and humorist)

Section IV: Good Leaders Know Where They Are Going

7. The leader has vision and foresight

"Foresight is the supreme attribute of a statesman. Foresight is the ability to recognize problems and to solve them in a manner beneficial in the short and long term." Thucydides (Ancient Greek historian)

"There is no more powerful engine driving an organization toward excellence and long range success than an attractive, worthwhile, achievable vision for the future, widely shared." Burt Nanus (Author of Visionary Leadership).

"A leader needs a clear point of view as to what the future holds." Sam Palmisano (Former CEO of IBM)

8. The leader translates that vision into clear, unambiguous goals for others

"Leadership is the capacity to translate vision into reality." Warren Bennis (Leadership professor at USC)

"Great leaders are almost always great simplifiers, who can cut through argument, debate and doubt to offer a solution everybody can understand." Colin Powell (US General and former Secretary of State)

"The most important role of any manager is to break down a situation into challenges a subordinate can handle. In essence, the manager absorbs a great deal of the ambiguity in the situation and gives much less ambiguous problems to others." Richard Rumelt (UCLA business school professor)

"Effective leaders don't have to be passionate. They don't have to be charming. They don't have to be brilliant…They don't have to be great speakers. What they must be is clear." Marcus Buckingham (Business book author)

Section V: Good Leaders Build a Culture That Reflects Their Values

9. Good leaders determine the appropriate values for their company

"When it comes to bringing values to life — to doing the good, right, and appropriate thing…we're always working at it, we're never totally there, and the challenge starts all over again with each new tomorrow." Eric Harvey and Steve Ventura (Business book co-authors)

"Never become wedded to what you make, but to the values the corporation stands for." Sam Palmisano (Former CEO of IBM)

"Values are like fingerprints. Nobody's are the same but you leave them all over everything you do." Elvis Presley (The King of Rock and Roll)

10. Good leaders build a sustainable company culture to support those values

"I came to see in my time at IBM, that culture isn't just one aspect of the game — it is the game." Lou Gerstner (Former CEO of IBM)

"Corporate culture is all important! It tells everyone in the company how to behave as an employee. It tells someone what is acceptable behavior and what is not. I can't personally talk to all 18,000 people in our company, but I can certainly clarify what the culture is and what our values are by being a personal representation of those values for all to see." Shelly Lazarus (CEO of Oglivy and Mather)

"For individuals, character is destiny. For organizations, culture is destiny." Tony Hsieh (CEO of Zappos)

"Throughout history, the mark of an enduring civilization has been that it has a common set of shared values." Professor Rufus Fears (History professor at the University of Oklahoma)

Section VI: Good Leaders Master the Management Fundamentals

11. Good leaders follow-up relentlessly

"You should never aspire to be a manager or an executive if you don't do follow-up. You won't be happy, and you won't do a good job, because that's what leaders do most of the time." Martin Zwilling (Author of Do You Have What It Takes to Be an Entrepreneur?)

"People respect what you inspect not what you expect." Lou Gerstner (Former CEO of IBM)

"People need to be reminded more often than they need to be instructed." Samuel Johnson (18th century English author)

"The fortune is in the follow-up." Unknown

12. Good leaders provide support and feedback

"The best way to inspire people to a superior performance is to convince them by everything you do and by your everyday attitude that you are wholeheartedly supporting them." Harold S. Geenen (Former Chairman of ITT)

"The lessons for leaders: your job is to provide resources and support that build the confidence of players in themselves, each other, the team, and the excellence of the surrounding system." Rosabeth Moss Kanter (Harvard Business School Professor)

"Show me a manager who ignores the art of praise, and I will show you a lousy manager. Praise is infinitely more productive than punishment – could anything be clearer?" Michael Abrashoff (Former Captain of the USS Benfold and author of It's Your Ship)

"The worst feedback I got was the feedback that I never got." Unknown millions of employees

Section VII: 8 Other Characteristics of Good Leaders

13. Good leaders are humble

"To possess self-confidence and humility at the same time is called maturity." Jack Welch (Former CEO of GE)

"Success is probably the worst problem for an entrepreneur. As people get too successful, they stop learning." Ken Olsen (Founder of Digital Equipment Corporation).

"I have seen ego destroy so many people in so many businesses. You have to be humble and open to learning every day." Glen Senk (CEO of Urban Outfitters)

"The idiot is bound by his pride. It always has to be his way. This is also true of the person who is deceptive or doing things wrong; he always tries to justify himself. A person who is bright in regard to his spiritual life is humble. He accepts what others tell him - criticism, ideas - and he works with them." Father Arenios (As quoted in Boomerang by Michael Lewis)

14. Good leaders are honest with themselves

"The first principle is that you must not fool yourself, and you are the easiest person to fool." Richard Feynman (Nobel Prize winning physicist)

"Two elements of successful leadership: a willingness to be wrong and an eagerness to admit it." Seth Godin (American entrepreneur and author)

"Maria Teresa (Archduchess of Austria who lived from 1717 to 1780) had one advisor, Emmanuel Count Sylva-Tarouca, who was employed as her official critic. It was his job to tell the Archduchess all of her mistakes." Jonathan Steinberg (Professor of history at the University of Pennsylvania)

"I have many faults. But, being wrong is not one of them." Jimmy Hoffa (American labor union leader)

15. Good leaders possess self-control

"The key to leadership is self-control: primarily, the mastery of pride, which is more difficult to subdue than a wild lion ("If you cannot swallow your pride, you cannot lead."); secondarily, the mastery of anger, which is more difficult to defeat than the greatest wrestler." Genghis Khan (Founder of the Mongol Empire in the 13th century)

"To conquer one's spirit, abandon anger, and be modest in victory... whoever can do this I compare not to the greatest of men but to a god." Cicero (Roman orator, philosopher and statesman)

"Eternal fame is deserved only by him who will have victory over himself." Orpheus (Legendary musician and poet in Ancient Greece)

"By swallowing evil words unsaid, no one has ever harmed his stomach." Winston Churchill (British Prime Minister during World War II)

"Don't do things in anger: 'You can always tell a man to go to hell tomorrow.'" Warren Buffett (Legendary investor and CEO of Berkshire Hathaway)

"'*Is*' is not the same as '*ought*' – simply because you can do something doesn't mean you should. David Hume (Scottish philosopher)

16. Good leaders have persistence and an unrelenting drive to succeed

"A Level V Executive [the best leader] has an unwavering resolve to do what must be done." Jim Collins (Author of <u>Good to Great</u>)

"The truly great players are those who push themselves and discipline themselves to do things right all the time, to be the best they can be. It is the same way in life. The person who is dedicated and can discipline himself will be the one who succeeds most often." Tony Dungy (Super Bowl-winning football coach)

"When I thought I couldn't go on, I forced myself to keep going. My success is based on persistence, not luck." Estée Lauder (Founder of Estée Lauder companies)

"Crucial qualities for success needed in a long war – tenacious persistence and absolute determination." James MacGregor Burns (Professor of government at Williams College)

17. Good leaders are decisive and action – oriented

"Be willing to make decisions. That's the most important quality in a good leader." George S. Patton Jr. (US General in World War II)

"The one word that makes a good manager -- decisiveness." Lee Iacocca (Former CEO of Chrysler Corporation)

"Leadership without the discipline of execution is incomplete and ineffective. Without the ability to execute, all other attributes of leadership become hollow." Ram Charan and Larry Bossidy (Co-authors of Execution: The Discipline of Getting Things Done)

18. But, no, good leaders do not need to be miracle workers

"Leaders spend so much time, money and attention striving to be the best or world-class. As a result, they often skip the step of just being good at leadership. But, it is infinitely better to be a good leader in fact than to be a great leader in fiction." David Shedd (Me)

"Do not let the best be the enemy of the good." Voltaire (18th century French philosopher and writer)

"To be a success, you need a reasonable degree of intelligence, a strong work ethic, the ability to get along with others, a desire to build something important, and the ability to keep one's ego in check." David Rubenstein (Wharton business school professor)

"In short, a good manager is nothing more or less than a good and well educated person." Matthew Stewart (Author of The Management Myth)

19. And a little bit of luck always helps

"But ability does not guarantee achievement, nor is achievement proportional to ability. And so it is important to always keep in mind the other term in the equation – the role of chance." Leonard Mlodinow (US physicist and author)

"Circumstance and luck matter. You have to have a plan of your own, and drive and skill. But being in the right place and in the right circumstances matters." Mark Little (Senior executive at GE)

"I want generals who are really good and really lucky." Napoleon Bonaparte (Emperor of France from 1804 to 1815)

20. As does a sense of humor

"Humor, used skillfully, greases the management wheels. It reduces hostility, deflects criticism, relieves tension, improves morale, and helps communicate difficult messages." Fabio Sala (Consultant with the Hay Group)

"A sense of humor is part of the art of leadership, of getting along with people, of getting things done." Dwight D. Eisenhower (34th President of the United States)

"The key to being a good manager is keeping the people who hate me away from those who are still undecided." Casey Stengel (Famed manager of the New York Yankees)

Chapter 3: A Successful Company Has a Winning Team

Section I: A Winning Team is Well-Led

21. Good leaders build team spirit

"Team Spirit is the eagerness to sacrifice personal interests and glory for the good and greatness of the team. It means putting "we" ahead of "me."" John Wooden (Famed UCLA basketball coach)

"Winning teams…have a cohesiveness and common focus on shared values and a commitment to reaching their shared and personal goals." Martin Zwilling (Author of <u>Do You Have What It Takes to Be an Entrepreneur?</u>)

"All players at the top [soccer] clubs are more or less as good as each other; the trick is to achieve team spirit." Jose Mourinho (Coach of Real Madrid soccer team)

22. Good leaders ensure that the right people are on the team

"First get the right people on the bus and the wrong people off the bus – build a superior executive team." Jim Collins (Author of <u>Good to Great</u>)

"Hire well, manage little." Warren Buffett (Legendary investor and CEO of Berkshire Hathaway)

"In too many companies, poor performers are tolerated. These 'C' players are needed so that the 'B' players can convince themselves that they are 'A' players." Sheldon Harris (Former President of Cold Stone Creamery)

23. Good leaders support and develop these right people

"Treat a man as he is and he will remain as he is; treat a man as he can and should be and he will become as he can and should be." Johann Wolfgang von Goethe (German writer, artist, and scientist)

"Before you fire someone who is not performing, what did you do as a leader to help them get an A?" Ken Blanchard (Author of The One Minute Manager)

"You have to treat your employees like your customers." Herb Kelleher (Former CEO of Southwest Airlines)

"Stop acting as if you are managing you. This is the 'Golden Rule Fallacy'. You are leading and managing people who are different from you and thus need to be managed differently than you would want to be managed." Marshall Goldsmith (Leadership coach and author of What Got You Here Won't Get You There)

"Fail to honor people, they fail to honor you." Lao Tzu (Ancient Chinese philosopher)

24. Good leaders focus relentlessly on the team's success

"Leaders must teach those under their supervision that the team's success is their own personal success." John Wooden (Famed UCLA basketball coach)

"'How can I help you to be successful?' This is the one question to ask your staff 20 times a day." Manny Fernandez (Management consultant at KPMG).

"As a leader, don't worry about the level of individual prominence you have achieved; worry about the individuals you have helped become better people." Clayton Christensen (Professor at Harvard Business School)

"We must consider our subjects' good before our own." Louis XIV (French king)

25. Good leaders are modest (even self-effacing)

"The great leader speaks little. He never speaks carelessly. He works without self-interest and leaves no trace. When all is finished, the people say: 'We did it ourselves.'" Lao-tzu (Ancient Chinese philosopher)

"See everything; overlook a great deal; correct a little."   Pope John XXIII (Roman Catholic Pope)

"A good leader takes a little more than his share of the blame, a little less than his share of the credit." Arnold H. Glasgow (American psychologist)

26. Good leaders do not over-manage

"Managers frequently complain to me about the fact that subordinates 'nowadays' won't take responsibility. I have been interested to note how often these same managers keep a constant surveillance over the day-to-day performance of subordinates, sometimes two or three levels below themselves." Douglas McGregor (MIT management professor as quoted in 1960).

"How arrogant to think that someone evolves from a "C" player to an "A" or "B" player because of anything that we do. It is more likely that micro-managing and not giving them autonomy stopped them." Shirley Beagle (Businessperson)

"Nowadays, the most effective managers work hard at showing people how to find their own solutions, and then get out of their way." D. Michael Abrashoff (Former Captain of the USS Benfold)

"It is amazing how someone's IQ seems to double as soon as you give them responsibility and indicate that you trust them." Tim Ferriss (Author of The 4-Hour Workweek)

"We don't have as many managers as we should, but we would rather have too few than too many." Larry Page (Founder and CEO of Google)

Section II: The 10 Characteristics of Winning Teams

27. Winning teams are aligned to achieve their objectives

"All organizations are perfectly aligned to get the results they get." Arthur W. Jones (Businessperson)

"The team with the best players does not always win. The team with the most alignment and commitment to each other will often win." Mike Romley (American entrepreneur)

"I'm becoming more and more convinced that you can improve the performance of almost any organization by tightening the alignment of its people, plans and practices around a shared purpose." George Bradt (Author of The New Leaders' 100 Day Action Plan)

28. Winning teams (and their members) are accountable for their results

"Accountability consists of clear standards, ways of measuring progress to the standards and most important, consequences for failure. The more we are able to say: 'It's not my fault.' The more we keep being mediocre." Anthony Booker (Mayor of Newark, New Jersey)

"When someone does not produce and does not improve, it is not fair to them to keep them on. They cannot possibly enjoy not being successful, and it is arrogant on our part to believe that they could not be successful doing something else." Michael Lombardo and Robert Eichinger (Authors of The Leadership Machine)

"The man who takes responsibility for results, no matter how junior, is in the most literal sense of the phrase, 'top management.'" Peter Drucker (Author and management theorist)

"Let everyone sweep in front of his own door, and the whole world will be clean." Johann Wolfgang von Goethe (German writer, artist, and scientist)

29. Winning teams allow and encourage autonomy within the accountability

"It is better to beg for forgiveness than to ask for permission." Anonymous

"Overcome the desire to tell subordinates how to do it. Refrain from detailing how a task is to be accomplished. Demand a solution, not the solution." Leonard Wong (Professor of military strategy at the Army War College)

"Knowledge workers must be autonomous...workers should be asked to think through their own work plans and then to submit them. What am I going to focus on? What results can be expected for which I should be held accountable? By what deadline?" Peter Drucker (Author and management theorist)

30. The members of the team are engaged and motivated to win

"Let's look at employee engagement first. It goes without saying that no company, small or large, can win over the long run without energized employees who believe in the mission and understand how to achieve it." Jack and Suzy Welch (Authors of <u>Winning</u>)

"The number one element of great management – make sure people know what is expected of them so they can engage." Gallup Research

"There is a rich body of evidence that intrinsic motivation is often supported by three key factors: autonomy, mastery and purpose. High effort and performance often result from designing jobs to provide freedom of choice, the chance to develop one's skills and expertise and the opportunity to do work that matters. Evidence also supports the importance of a fourth factor: a sense of connection with other people." Daniel H. Pink (Author of <u>Drive: The Surprising Truth About What Motivates Us</u>)

"You will never have higher engagement from your customers than you have with your employees."   Mark Herbert (Author and management consultant on employee engagement)

31. The members of winning teams are decisive and make it happen

"There is no more effective way to destroy leadership potential of young officers and noncommissioned officers than to deny them opportunities to make decisions appropriate for their assignments." Frederick Kroesen (US Army General)

"Decisions should be made at the lowest possible level where the person making the decision has full accountability for the decision." Ed Shedd (My dad)

"Any commander who fails to exceed his authority is not of much use to his subordinates." Arleigh Burke (Admiral in the US Navy during World War II and the Korean War)

32. Winning teams renounce bureaucracy in all its forms

"More than anything, the bureaucratic mind-set is characterized by the failure to take initiative." Rufus Fears (History professor at the University of Oklahoma)

"Most managers were trained to be the thing they most despise - bureaucrats." Alvin Toffler (American writer and futurist)

"We would rather suffer the visible costs of a few bad decisions than incur the many invisible costs that come from decisions made too slowly – or not at all – because of a stifling bureaucracy." Warren Buffett (Legendary investor and CEO of Berkshire Hathaway)

"The only thing that saves us from bureaucracy is its inefficiency." Jason Jennings (Author of Less is More)

33. Honesty and candor are prevalent within winning teams

"Honesty is the first chapter in the book of wisdom." Thomas Jefferson (3rd President of the United States)

"Lack of candor is the biggest dirty little secret in business." Jack Welch (Former CEO of GE)

"To paraphrase Warren Buffett, honesty and candor allow everyone to clearly see 'who is swimming naked.' With that, the real issues and challenges can be brought to the front, be recognized by everyone, and be addressed." David Shedd

"People sometimes stumble over the truth, but usually they pick themselves up and hurry about their business." Winston Churchill (British Prime Minister during World War II)

34. Listening and communication are hallmarks of winning teamwork

"Successful people ask better questions, and as a result, they get better answers." Anthony Robbins (American self-help author and motivational speaker)

"Communication doesn't take place until people: Hear or see what you say. Understand it. Believe it. Believe you mean it. Remember it. Internalize it. And begin to use it themselves." Vince Lombardi (Super Bowl-winning football coach)

"One of my roles as CEO is to be the chief listener. I don't believe that the model is any longer that there are a few really smart people at the top of the pyramid that make all the strategic decisions. It is much more about being all around the enterprise, and looking for people with great ideas and passionate points of view that are anchored to the business and connected to things our customers care about." Brian Dunn (CEO of Best Buy)

"It's not always what we say; often it's what we allow the other person to say. By listening, we gain trust and make other people feel more comfortable with us." Rick Pitino (College basketball coach)

"I speak and speak, but the listener retains only the words he is expecting." Marco Polo (Italian explorer)

35. Mutual support and recognition are pervasive within winning teams

"Napoleon created rewards such as the Legion of Honor to motivate his men. One of his advisors said, 'but it is bauble [trinkets], Sire.' Napoleon replied, "Men are ruled by almost nothing else." Paul Johnson (Napoleon biographer)

"One of the main reasons why people end relationships in life or work is that they receive limited, if any, genuine praise or recognition for their contributions." Robert K. Cooper (Strategic advisor to CEO's)

"The deepest human need is the need to be appreciated." William James (U.S. psychologist)

"Recognition is the most powerful currency you have, and it costs you nothing." Jessica Herrin (CEO of Stella and Dot)

"In the end, everybody wants recognition and respect."   Michael Bloomberg (Mayor of New York City)

36. A winning team constantly learns and improves

"I don't have to be brighter than everybody else, I don't have to have more money than everybody else...I just have to outlearn everybody. And that's a very easy thing to do because almost no one is focused on continual learning. If you spend even one hour each day learning, and then the rest of the day applying what you learnt, you would revolutionize any industry. You would be a top-performer." Simon Reynolds (Entrepreneur, business coach, and founder of Photon Group)

"What the best may have, above all, is the capacity to learn and change – and to do so faster than everyone else." Atul Gawande (American physician and author)

"In times of change, learners inherit the earth, while those that know it all find themselves beautifully equipped to deal with a world that no longer exists." Eric Hoffer (American social writer)

"It ain't what you don't know that gets you in trouble. But what you know for sure that just ain't so."   Mark Twain (19th century American author and humorist)

"When you lose, don't lose the lesson." Tenzin Gyatso (14th Dalai Lama)

"Learn from the mistakes of others - you can never live long enough to make them all yourself." Eleanor Roosevelt (First Lady of the United States from 1933 – 1945)

Chapter 4: A Successful Company Performs

Section I: The Company is Focused on Profitable Opportunities

37. The company focuses on and exploits profitable niches

"Highly focused companies – those with a small number of strongly positioned businesses – did much better than diversified companies over the last decade. Suggestions to match these successful companies include: reduce rather than extend the scope of your business; find profitable opportunities within the boundaries of current operations; search ceaselessly for ways to improve the performance of the core business." Bain and Company study

"When a management with a reputation for brilliance tackles a business with a reputation for bad economics, it is the reputation of the business that remains intact." Warren Buffett (Legendary investor and CEO of Berkshire Hathaway)

38. Business acumen is prevalent throughout the company

"Business acumen can help you cut through the complexity to make the right decisions every day." Ram Charan (Business leadership consultant)

"If you are doing anything that you think a customer would not be willing to pay a premium for – think twice before doing it." Carlos Brito (CEO of Anheuser-Busch In-Bev)

"Wisdom is crucial to business success. But, wisdom is more than just information, data, or knowledge. Wisdom is the insight, vision and business acumen that allows a leader, a team, or an individual to see through the fog of their daily reality and understand what drives the success of their company." David Shedd

"It is better to learn how to prosper within markets than to fight against them." Arthur Laffer (Economist and business consultant)

39. There is a focus on and appreciation of the front line of the business

"You have to understand what is happening on the ground. You have to be able to see what works and what doesn't and to adapt quickly. Otherwise you'll spend years running plays that have no chance of succeeding." Jonathan Starr (Founder of Flagg Street Capital now running Abaarso Tech)

"The further you are from the combat, the dumber you are." David Petraeus (US General during the wars in Iraq and Afghanistan)

"Leaders should maintain contact with the front-lines and with customers. This allows for truthful information gathering unhindered by the filters (and personal agendas) of the different layers of management." Skills for Success: The Experts Show the Way

"The field is important, not the headquarters." Jack Welch (Former CEO of GE)

"Farming looks mighty easy when your plow is a pencil and you're a thousand miles from the corn field." Dwight D. Eisenhower (34th President of the United States)

40. The customer is appreciated

"If your CEO does not love customers and is not committed to delivering value, your venture will fail." Ken Morse (Serial entrepreneur, Co-founder of 3Com)

"The customer should be the center of any company's universe. A good product does not always get you there." Tom Steenburgh (Professor at Harvard Business School)

"Every decision is made by the person who has the power to make the decision — not the best person, the right person or the logical person. This person is our customer. If we influence this person, we make a difference. If we do not influence this person, we do not make a difference. Once we accept this basic fact of life, we can 'get on with life' and quit whining." Peter Drucker (Author and management theorist)

"A customer is not dependent on us, we are dependent on him. A customer is not an interruption of our work; he is the purpose of it." Leon Leonwood Bean (Founder of L.L. Bean retail store)

41. Customer service is a priority with the goal of true customer satisfaction

"Customers are often only satisfied because their expectations are so low and because no one else is doing any better. Perhaps, the customer service slogan should be: 'No Worse than the Competition.'" Ken Blanchard and Sheldon Bowles (Authors of Raving Fans)

"Zappos tries to see customer service not as a cost but as a powerful marketing tool." Tony Hsieh (CEO of Zappos)

"Customer service is not about reading from a script it is about resolving issues and ensuring client happiness." Drew J. Stevens (Sales and business development consultant)

"With effective customer satisfaction, you continue to remind your repeat customers of how smart they were to make the initial decision to buy from you." David Shedd

"How many customers did we fail to satisfy yesterday?" Howard Lester (Former owner of Williams – Sonoma)

42. The company balances both the short term and the long term

"If you study the root causes of business disasters, over and over you'll find this predisposition toward endeavors that offer immediate gratification." Clayton Christensen (Professor at Harvard Business School)

"No one will thank you for taking care of the present if you have neglected the future." Joel Barker (Author of Future Edge)

"Our real problem is not our strength today; it is rather the vital necessity of action today to ensure our strength tomorrow." Calvin Coolidge (30th President of the United States)

"When our long-term competitive position improves as a result of these unnoticeable actions, we describe the phenomenon as "widening the moat." And doing that is essential if we are to have the kind of business we want a decade or two from now. We always, of course, hope to earn more money in the short-term. But, when short-term and long-term conflict, 'widening the moat' must take precedence. If a management makes bad decisions in order to hit short-term earnings targets, and consequently gets behind the eight ball in terms of costs, customer satisfaction or brand strength, no amount of subsequent brilliance will overcome the damage that has been inflicted. Take a look at the dilemmas of managers in the auto and airline industries today as they struggle with the huge problems handed them by their predecessors." Warren Buffett (Legendary investor and CEO of Berkshire Hathaway)

Section II: Collectively, the Company Gets the Right Things Done

43. The team makes it happen, executing on its goals daily

"The difference between a company and its competitors is its ability to execute; this is the critical difference for success." Larry Bossidy and Ram Charan (Co-authors of Execution: The Discipline of Getting Things Done)

"Doing things the right way and following through on what you are supposed to do is the difference between being a championship team and being a mediocre one." Tony Dungy (Super Bowl-winning football coach)

"Sustained success is largely a matter of focusing regularly on the right things and making a lot of uncelebrated little improvements every day." Theodore Levitt (Marketing professor at Harvard Business School)

"Success for our company is not going to take a new strategy or an entirely new business model. Instead it's taking what we already do well and continuing to execute those strengths." Blake W. Nordstrom (CEO of Nordstrom)

44. The company and the team do what they say

"To build trust, you must do two things. First, say what you mean. Second, do what you say." Jack Welch (Former CEO of GE)

"Return calls and E-Mails in a timely way. That would put you 99.9% ahead of your competitors. People are shocked, people are in awe. They can't believe it. And we can't believe that people can't believe it because we think everybody should do it." Dan Gilbert (Founder of Quicken Loans)

45. The business is kept simple and repeatable processes are developed

"I would not give a fig for the simplicity on this side of complexity, but I would give my life for the simplicity on the other side of complexity." Oliver Wendell Holmes (US Supreme Court Justice)

"Most of what we call management today consists of making it difficult for people to get their work done." Peter Drucker (Author and management theorist)

"Make it as simple as possible, but no simpler." Albert Einstein (Nobel Prize winning physicist)

"Any intelligent fool can make things bigger, more complex, and more violent. It takes a touch of genius — and a lot of courage—to move in the opposite direction." E. F. Schumacher (British-based economist and economic thinker)

"Regularly ask yourself, your managers, and the whole company: 'Which of our current activities would we start now if they weren't already under way?' Then eliminate all the others." Heiche Bruch and Jochen I. Menges (Authors of "The Acceleration Trap")

"Process is important in every aspect of a business. You need to get the right outcome doing it the right way so that you could achieve the right outcome again and again." Philip Delves Broughton (Author of Ahead of the Curve: Two Years at Harvard Business School)

"You don't have the right processes if it takes exceptional people to do ordinary things or if it takes heroics to perform tasks that should be routine." Michael Hammer (Author of The Agenda)

"Success or failure often depends on getting the fundamentals correct in an ambiguous world." Tim Harford (Author of The Logic of Life).

46. The company is easy to work with and easy to buy from

"The customer wants to give you their money. By all means, help them to do so: be easy to do business with." David Shedd

"To build trust with your customers, be available, be the expert, and be accommodating." Josh Norman (Journalist)

"Always take a problem away from a customer. Don't ever hesitate to fix the problem even it is not your fault. Mimic the customer's own style, except if someone is angry – then let him vent." Unknown

"Legendary service is not about arguing over who is right or finding someone else to blame – it is about fixing the problem for the customer." Ken Blanchard (Author of the One Minute Manager)

Section III: Problem Solving and Decision Making are Effective

47. The team focuses on the important and relevant facts, facing reality

"One cognitive ability distinguished star performers from average: pattern recognition, the 'big picture' thinking that allows leaders to pick out the meaningful trends from a welter of information around them and to think strategically far into the future." Daniel Goleman (Author, psychologist, and science journalist writing about a study of top executives at fifteen large companies)

"As communication grows ever easier, the important thing is detecting whispers of useful information in a howling hurricane of noise." Schumpeter (Pseudonymous columnist in *The Economist)*

"Most companies explain away the brutal facts rather than having to confront the brutal facts head-on" Roger Connors et al (Authors of The Oz Principle)

"The following is always wrong: 'We're losing market share because our competitors are crazy and they are giving the product away.'" Jack Welch (Former CEO of GE)

"Troubled companies are typically in denial and can't understand why they're in trouble and why they need to change." Steve Miller (Author of The Turnaround Kid).

"Facts do not cease to exist because they are ignored." Aldous Huxley (English writer; author of Brave New World)

48. The team gets the viewpoints of all involved

"I also hope that my truth pleases you, because there are many truths, many truths. It's up to you to decide which is the true truth and analyze it afterwards." Ronaldo (Brazilian soccer player speaking to a Senate Commission investigating Brazil's 1998 World Cup loss)

"And the endeavor to ascertain these facts was a laborious task, because those who were eyewitnesses of the several events did not give the same reports about the same things, but reports varying according to their championship of one side of the other, or according to their recollections." Thucydides (Ancient Greek historian and author)

"There are three sides to every story: your side, my side and the truth. And no one is lying. Memories shared serve each differently." Robert Evans (Hollywood producer)

49. The company determines the root cause and defines well the problem

"In the time of the Middle Kingdom [in Ancient China], Confucius was asked by the emperor: 'What is the single most important advice you can give for ruling my kingdom?' Confucius replied: "First, you must define the problem.'" Confucius (Ancient Chinese philosopher)

"Defining a problem is the key to solving a problem. What you have to learn is that the other guy may have a different definition of the problem." Alfredo Cristiani (Former President of El Salvador)

"Spend spending relatively more time and effort on defining the problem and critical issues and relatively less time on finding solutions." Toyota management principle

"A problem well stated is a problem well solved." John Dewey (Early 20th century American educator)

"Unfortunately, an entire industry can get caught up in solving the wrong problems." Arthur Laffer (Economist and business consultant)

"Focusing on the right critical issues – no more than three to five, in most cases – is crucial to achieving success." Orit Gadiesh and Hugh MacArthur (Authors of Lessons from Private Equity any Company Can Use)

50. The company solves problems and makes decisions systematically

"I tell my MBA students that whenever you are going with your gut, you are doing something wrong. In most cases, you can actually figure it out. So, you should sit down and figure it out." Peter Cappelli (Management professor at Wharton business school)

"A decision without an alternative is a desperate gambler's throw, no matter how carefully thought through it might be." Peter Drucker (Author and management theorist)

"Think through the consequences of every business decision you make before you actually make it." Gary Vaynerchuk (Belarussian-American entrepreneur and author)

"We cannot solve problems by using the same kind of thinking we had when we created them." Albert Einstein (Nobel Prize winning physicist)

"Unlike in school, plagiarism should be encouraged. If someone else has a clever idea or way to solve your problem, by all means legally use it. "Not invented here" syndrome is just sheer arrogance." David Shedd

51. Biases are avoided in any way possible

"The person who frames the decision all too often makes the decision." Decision Theory maxim

"We should spend as much time looking for evidence that we are wrong as we spend searching for reasons we are correct." Leonard Mlodinow (US physicist and author)

"Most real life problems are large, messy, and difficult to define. When an expert tackles a problem, the problem is often redefined to fit into the expert's field. The problem solution then becomes the problem definition." Bruce Corson (Engineering and Design Consultant)

"He that is good with the hammer tends to think everything is a nail." Abraham Maslow (American professor of psychology)

"Guard against 'confirmation bias' by giving one team member the job of looking for flaws." Rita Gunther McGrath (Professor at Columbia Business School).

52. Decisions are made timely and solutions are implementable

"Decisiveness in decisions is vital. Make 80% of your decisions on the spot; 15% need to mature; 5% need not be made at all. <u>Skills for Success: The Experts Show the Way</u>

"Managers should make a decision no later than you need it, but as late as possible, because you will always have more information." Peter Drucker (Author and management theorist)

"Learn to make nonfatal or reversible decision as quickly as possible. Fast decisions preserve usable attention for what matters." Tim Ferriss (Author of <u>The 4-Hour Workweek</u>)

"Big problems are rarely solved with commensurately big solutions. Instead, they are most often solved by a sequence of small solutions." Chip and Dan Heath (Co-authors of <u>Switch</u> and <u>Made to Stick</u>)

"Everybody was looking for the home run that solved all of the accidents. The more we got down to it, the things that had the biggest impact were base hits. Ed Soliday (United Airlines executive discussing improving aviation safety).

"Without proper implementation…even the best plan is useless." Unknown

Chapter 5: A Successful Company Improves and Evolves

Section I: The Company is Focused on Daily, Continuous Improvement

53. Continuous improvement is fundamental

"The competitor to be feared is one who never bothers about you at all, but goes on making his own business better all the time." Henry Ford (Founder of Ford Motor Company)

"First and foremost what used to consistently keep me bothered nights and days alike is how to keep the work force motivated to stick to the objective of continuous improvement, to always remain constructively dissatisfied with the end result. In my view, this is what keeps a company competitive into the future. It is a culture characteristic that has to be instilled and sustained without the constant need to micromanage business results from the COO and/or the executive staff." B Mitchell White (Advisor to COO's)

54. Improve daily

"Every day, in countless ways, the competitive position of each of our businesses grows either weaker or stronger. If we are delighting customers, eliminating unnecessary costs, and improving our products and services, we gain strength. But, if we treat customers with indifference or tolerate bloat, our businesses will wither. On a daily basis, the effects of our actions are imperceptible; cumulatively, though, their consequences are enormous." Warren Buffett (Legendary investor and CEO of Berkshire Hathaway)

"Walk before you run. Small changes every day in areas within the team's control and where buy-in is strong is the best place to start and build momentum." Steven Bonacorsi (Operational improvement consultant)

When you improve a little each day, eventually big things occur… Don't look for the quick, big improvement. Seek the small improvement one day at a time. That's the only way it happens- and when it happens, it lasts." John Wooden (Famed UCLA basketball coach)

Section II: The Company is Effective at Managing Change

55. Change is recognized as being both necessary and inevitable

"It is not the strongest of the species that survives, nor the most intelligent, but the one most responsive to change." Charles Darwin (19th century English naturalist)

"To improve is to change; to be perfect is to change often." Winston Churchill (British Prime Minister during World War II)

"Change happens all the time and always will happen. And change is not always in the best interest of everyone. Some people will lose. But, without the change, everyone would lose." Howard Perlstein (Business transformation consultant)

"The only thing you know for sure is that if you do nothing, then nothing will happen. Nothing will change." Bill Watkins (Former CEO of Seagate Technology)

"It is not necessary to change. Survival is not mandatory." W. Edwards Deming (20th century American expert on quality)

56. Change is also acknowledged as being difficult even painful

"Only 30% of executive surveyed consider their change programs to be successful." *McKinsey and Company survey*

"Change is so difficult because discipline and self-control are exhaustible resources. When changing, we simply require too much of people, too much discipline, too much self-control. And so they give up and fail." Chip and Dan Heath (Co-authors of Switch and Made to Stick)

"The only person who likes change is a baby with a wet diaper." Mark Twain (19th century American author and humorist)

57. The company faces reality and sees the need for change early

"Sometimes the most difficult act of leadership is not fighting the enemy; it's telling yourself and your friends that it is time to change." Bill Gates (Founder and former CEO of Microsoft)

"Each corporate crisis is unique, though one thing they have in common is hubris (pride) that blinds the senior managers to changes in the marketplace." Steve Miller (Author of The Turnaround Kid)

"The fall from greatness, though, was from lost discipline driven by a failure of leadership to listen, to continuously renew, to act sooner, and to keep the strategy fresh and great along the way. Like the popular buy and hold investment strategy, some of the companies seemed happy with average performance and overly reluctant to fix what wasn't (clearly) broken." Arthur Laffer (Economist and business consultant)

"When the pace of change outside an organization becomes greater than the pace of change inside the organization, the end is near." John R. Walter (Former President, ATT)

"If you are failing at your job, figure out what your successor will do, and then do it before he is given the chance". Gary Wendt (Former CEO of GE Capital)

58. The company works hard to escape "old thinking"

"Chains of habit are too light to be felt until they are too heavy to be broken" Warren Buffett (Legendary investor and CEO of Berkshire Hathaway)

"The difficulty lies not in the new ideas, but in escaping the old ones." John Maynard Keynes (British economist)

"You can clutch the past so tightly to your chest that it leaves your arms too full to embrace the present." Jan Glidewell (American author and journalist) "Companies [are biased] to leverage what they have put in place to succeed in the past, instead of guiding them to create the capabilities they'll need in the future. If we knew the future would be exactly the same as the past, then that approach would be fine. But if the future's different—and it almost always is— then it's the wrong thing to do." Clayton Christensen (Professor at Harvard Business School)

"The great danger in times of turbulence is not the turbulence; it is to act with yesterday's logic." Peter Drucker (Author and management theorist)

59. The change reflects the change in the external environment

"The industrial landscape is already littered with the remains of once successful companies that could not adapt their strategic vision to altered conditions of competition." Ralph Abernathy (American civil rights leader)

"Do not confuse the stability of your mindset with the stability in the environment. Your mindset may be stable while the business environment is tremendously unstable." Ellen Langer (Professor of psychology at Harvard University)

"There are a lot of businesses struggling to grow today. But most aren't really trying. They keep doing more of what they've always done, and hoping for a better result! They don't accept that trends go in new directions, causing markets to shift. When markets shift, those who follow the trends do far better than those stuck trying to defend their past strategies." Adam Hartung (Consultant and author on business growth and Innovation)

"Should you find yourself in a chronically leaking boat, energy devoted to changing vessels is likely to be more productive than energy devoted to patching leaks." Warren Buffett (Legendary investor and CEO of Berkshire Hathaway)

60. A successful change involves the individuals on the team

"Change is a threat when done to me, but an opportunity when done by me." Rosabeth Moss Kantor (Professor at Harvard Business School)

"A change initiative can go wrong when the fix is determined by the experts and then rolled out to the whole system. This ignores people and their potential for contribution and engagement. So the answer is to go to one plant, do the work there, make it a star performer, and then apply it to other plants. Once one plant takes it on, and there is a dramatic improvement, people say 'Wow, what did you do?' Then the change initiative can be replicated throughout the whole system." Adam Farber (Partner at Boston Consulting Group)

"In practice, however, relationships and dignity are essential to making the most difficult changes and minimizing the fall-out from the changes." Howard Perlstein (Business transformation consultant)

"People often resent change when they have no involvement in how it should be implemented. So, contrary to popular belief, people do not resist change, they resist being controlled." Ken Blanchard (Author of The One Minute Manager)

61. Any change emphasizes changing the mindset and behavior of the people

"The hardest part of a business transformation is changing the culture – the mindset and instincts of the people in the company." Lou Gerstner (Former CEO of IBM)

"The core of the matter is always about changing the behavior of people, and behavior change happens in highly successful situations mostly by speaking to people's feelings… In highly successful change efforts, people find ways to help other see the problems or solutions in ways that influence emotions, not just thought. John Kotter and Dan Cohen (Authors of The Heart of Change)

"People need to want to change. People convinced against their will are of the same opinion still." Phil Batchelor (City Manager of Vallejo, California)

62. The change (even when big) is broken down into small, achievable steps

"A small win reduces importance ("this is no big deal"), reduces demands ("that's all that needs to be done"), and raises the perceived skill levels ("I can do at least that"). All three of these factors will tend to make change easier and more self-sustaining." Karl Weick (Professor at the University of Michigan business school)

"Incremental change is better than ambitious failure... Success feeds on itself." Tony Schwartz (Author of The Power of Full Engagement)

"Small simple steps are the path of least resistance for change." Richard Fast (Canadian entrepreneur and author)

"You can't move so fast that you try to change [a situation] faster than people can accept it. That doesn't mean you do nothing, but it means that you do the things that need to be done according to priority." Eleanor Roosevelt (First Lady of the United States from 1933 to 1945)

63. But, the change initiative does not take on a life of its own

"One challenge in change is the 'River Kwai Syndrome'. In the movie The Bridge on the River Kwai, the colonel was so focused on maintaining the morale of his men by building the bridge that he forgot the more important issue was to win the war. To the leaders of a change initiative, the success of the change initiative can often become the goal in and of itself, thus overshadowing the more important issue: improving the overall business." David Shedd

"Be careful what you measure, you may get it – and it may kill you. Complete focus on a metric is likely to improve the metric, but not necessarily the business." Michael Hammer (Author of The Agenda)

Chapter 6: A Successful Company Grows

Section I: The First Step in Growth is to Satisfy Current Customers

64. The business evolves and grows with its good customers

"The easiest person to sell to is your current customer." Steve Harrison (Publicity and marketing expert)

"More customers are lost to apathy after the sale than poor service or quality. Many experts suggest it costs six times more to sell something to a new customer than to an existing customer." Martin Zwilling (Author of Do You Have What It Takes to Be an Entrepreneur?)

"Companies need to be closer to their final customers in order to hold them, to up-sell them and to cross-sell them and to garner high margin follow-on sales. They need to be closer to serve them quickly and accurately. They need to be closer to drive out the huge costs and inefficiencies, the redundant work and piles of inventory, that clutter existing channels." Michael Hammer (Author of The Agenda)

"All too often businesses over emphasize the importance of new customer sales as a key to building a business. While this is and continues to be an integral component of business growth, real and sustainable growth occurs when a business leverages its relationships– team, customer, suppliers, ownership–in a strategically focused manner to retain and expand the ones it already has." David Cooke (Sales coach and sales trainer)

65. This success with current customers brings new customers

"If you do build a great experience, customers tell each other about that. Word of mouth is very powerful." Jeff Bezos (Founder and CEO of Amazon)

"Customers are three times more likely to trust peer opinions over advertising for purchasing decisions." Jupiter Research

"Word of mouth is more believable than traditional advertising." Tom Farley (Head of marketing at Ford Motor Company)

"The best marketing and advertising comes via personal referral." Dave Opton (Founder of ExecuNet)

Section II: A Realizable Strategy is Developed and Implemented

66. The first step in any strategy is to evaluate the current business

"The granddaddy of all mistakes is competing to be the best, going down the same path as everybody else and thinking that somehow you can achieve better results."   Michael Porter (Harvard Business School professor and author of Competitive Strategy)

"Practice purposeful abandonment of businesses – constantly assess which businesses are good for today and which businesses will be good for tomorrow. 'If you were not in this business today, would you invest the resources to enter it?' If the answer is no, then what are you going to do about it." Peter Drucker (Author and management theorist)

"It's painful, expensive, time-consuming, stressful and ultimately pointless to work overtime to preserve your dying business model…Again and again the winners are individuals and organizations that spot opportunities in the next thing, as opposed to those that would demonize, marginalize or illegalize (is that a word?) it."   Seth Godin (American entrepreneur and author)

67. The growth strategy is directed towards the future trends in the market

"Creative destruction is an easy excuse to avoid blaming leaders for failures caused by their unwillingness to recognize trends and take actions to invest in them which will create winning businesses." Adam Hartung (Consultant and author on business growth and innovation)

"A good hockey player plays where the puck is. A great hockey player plays where the puck is going to be." Wayne Gretzky ("The Great One" - famed ice hockey player)

"No sensible decision can be made any longer without taking into account not only the world as it is, but the world as it will be." Graham Speechley (British management consultant)

"You can't stop the waves, but you can learn to surf." Jon Kabat-Zinn (Professor of medicine and mindfulness meditation)

68. The company seeks out profitable niches

"Be focused like a hedgehog. With what products and in what markets, can you be deeply passionate about what you are doing, be the best in the world, and be able to make a profit and drive your economic engine?" Jim Collins (Author of Good to Great)

"The first challenge in strategy is picking the right thing to do. Pick the right industry, one with a sound structure, where your chances of making a profit are highest. This is where good strategy begins." Philip Delves Broughton (Author of Ahead of the Curve: Two Years at Harvard Business School)

"Focus on making the competition irrelevant by creating a leap in value for buyers and your company, thereby opening up new and uncontested market space." W. Chan Kim and Renee Mauborgne (Authors of Blue Ocean Strategy)

"You've got to look for a gap, where competitors in a market have grown lazy and lost contact with the readers or the viewers." Rupert Murdoch (Media mogul)

"In marketing, you cannot make a perfect storm, but you can find one." Seth Godin (American entrepreneur and author)

69. Having a competitive advantage is paramount

"For business strategy, you want to focus on competitive advantage. But, take it one step further. You want to focus on not going where you have a competitive disadvantage." Phillip Delves Broughton (Author of Ahead of the Curve: Two Years at Harvard Business School)

"If you don't have a competitive advantage, don't compete." Jack Welch (Former CEO of GE)

"The chief task of a good general is to force his enemies to give battle when he is superior to them, but not to be forced himself to do this when his forces are inferior." Plutarch (Ancient Greek historian)

"Don't dance where the elephants play." German proverb

70. The strategy specifically addresses what the company will not do

"Developing and executing an effective business strategy is all about choosing what not to do among the myriad of opportunities available." Michael Porter (Harvard Business School Professor and author of Competitive Strategy)

"The heart of strategy is being able to tell what you are not going to do. Telling what you're going to do is easy but telling what you are not going to do – like when you are going to say 'no' to your customer – is much harder." Denis Minev (Head of development in the Brazilian state of Amazonas)

"A company is more likely to die of indigestion from too much opportunity than starvation from too little." David Packard (Co-founder of Hewlett-Packard)

"Courage often consists as much in refraining to do, as in doing." Farmer's Almanac

71. The strategic plan is implementable in the marketplace

"There is a maxim; 80% strategy with 100% execution will win over 100% strategy with 80% execution." Eugene Lee (American businessperson)

"The biggest reason CEO's fail is not bad strategy, but bad implementation of their strategy." Ram Charan (Leadership consultant; as reported in *Fortune* magazine)

"No plan survives contact with the enemy." Helmuth von Moltke (Prussian Field Marshall)

"In real life, strategy is actually very straightforward. You pick a general direction and implement like hell. Jack Welch (Former CEO of GE)

"Great companies lay out strategies that are believable and executable. These strategies are long on detail and short on vision." Lou Gerstner (Former CEO of IBM)

"Everyone has a plan until they get hit." Mike Tyson (American heavyweight champion boxer)

"However beautiful the strategy, you should occasionally look at the results." Winston Churchill (British Prime Minister during World War II)

Section III: Innovation is Managed Well

72. The company commits to a strategy of innovation

"We live in a world where the returns on incrementalism are going down and the returns on real innovation are going up." Gary Hamel (Professor at London Business School)

"Innovation is both a strategy and a result. You have to commit to the strategy of creating innovation, but, the vast majority of innovation is really a result. You are looking to create a specific result or breakthrough. You have to embrace creativity, innovation and the right culture in order to get there." Michael Howe (Former CEO of MinuteClinic)

73. Innovation has a definite goal – solving a customer problem

"I never perfected an invention that I did not think about in terms of the services it might give others. I find out what the world needs, then I proceed to invent." Thomas Edison (American inventor)

"Entrepreneurs should be driven to solve a valuable problem for customers." Ken Morse (Serial entrepreneur, Co-founder of 3Com)

"Innovation is the match between a solution and a need, connected in a novel way." Christian Terwiesch (Professor at Wharton business school)

74. Brainstorming and original thought are required

"Creativity is the power to connect the seemingly unconnected." William Plomer (South African writer)

"Look outside your group. An idea mundane (and seemingly intuitive) in one group can be a valuable insight in another." Ronald Burt (Author of The Social Origins of Good Ideas)

"Pay attention to what's happening on the fringe of your market and plan from the future back to the present." Adam Hartung (Consultant and author on business growth and innovation)

"Too much experience within a field may restrict creativity because you know so well how things should be done that you are unable to escape to come up with new ideas." Edward de Bono (Consultant on creative thinking)

"You won't make change by benchmarking the Fortune 500. You have to challenge dogma, explore the fringe and experiment." Gary Hamel (Professor at London Business School)

75. A culture of innovation flourishes from the bottom up

"In a survey by McKinsey of 600 executives, those at the top thought the main reason why their company wasn't innovative was that it didn't have enough of the right people. Lower level management held a markedly different view – that the company had the right people, but the culture kept them from innovating as they should." Geoff Colvin (Author of Talent is Overrated)

"Innovation that happens from the top down tends to be orderly but dumb. Innovation that happens from the bottom up tends to be chaotic but smart." Curtis Carlson (CEO of SRI International)

"The ultimate freedom for creative groups is the freedom to experiment with new ideas. Some skeptics insist that innovation is expensive. In the long run, innovation is cheap. Mediocrity is expensive – and autonomy can be the antidote. Tom Kelly (General Manager, IDEO)

"The desire to do something because you find it deeply satisfying and personally challenging inspires the highest levels of creativity, whether it's in the arts, sciences, or business." Teresa Amabile (Harvard University professor)

76. Mistakes and mis-starts are tolerated

"Companies that want to compete on innovation are well-advised to become more tolerant of errors in practice and develop better methods for capturing the lessons from mistakes." Paul J.H. Schoemaker (Author of Brilliant Mistakes)

"There are two sides to every coin...As soon as you say, 'failure is not an option,' you've just said, 'innovation is not an option.'" Seth Godin (American entrepreneur and author)

"I failed my way to success." Thomas Edison (American inventor)

"To be innovative, you have to be willing to fail and have a culture that allows you to fail. If you don't accept failure people won't take the appropriate risk." Jeff Kindler (CEO of Pfizer)

"Recently, I was asked if I was going to fire an employee who made a mistake that cost the company $600,000. 'No, I replied, I just spent $600,000 training him.'" Thomas J. Watson (Founder of IBM)

Section IV: New Product and Service Development Creates Growth

77. Product development focuses on what customers truly want and value

"The lesson Google and Apple are teaching us is that companies must have a good idea of the future, and then send their product development and marketing in that direction." Adam Hartung (Consultant and author on business growth and innovation)

"Your customers face new problems, so give them new solutions." Geoff Colvin (Author of Talent is Overrated)

"Creating demand is hard. Filling demand is much easier. Don't create a product, and then seek someone to sell it to. Find a market – define your customers – then find or develop a product for them." Tim Ferriss (Author of The 4-Hour Workweek)

"It doesn't matter what I think, it matters what the customer thinks." Bill Harrison (Publicity and marketing expert)

"Don't make the mistake of looking at market needs or requests as an afterthought to verify what's already been planned." Martin Zwilling (Author of Do You Have What It Takes to Be an Entrepreneur?)

78. Design is important – effective, simple and customer-friendly

"Good design…combines technology, cognitive science, human need, and beauty to produce something that the world didn't know it was missing." Paola Antonelli (Curator of architecture and design, Museum of Modern Art)

"Never compromise on usability. Regard usability as a non-negotiable essential characteristic of the design of your user experiences, always." Godfrey Parkin (British management consultant)

"A designer knows he has achieved perfection not when there is nothing left to add, but when there is nothing left to take away." Antoine de Saint-Exupery (French author of The Little Prince)

"That has been one of my mantras – focus and simplicity. Simple can be harder than complex; you have to work hard to get your thinking clean to make it simple. But it is worth it in the end because once you get there, you can move mountains." Steve Jobs (Founder and former CEO of Apple)

79. Product development is fast, if not perfect

"Kodak executives…suffered from a mentality of perfect products, rather than the high-tech mindset of make it, launch it, fix it." Rosabeth Moss Kantor (Harvard Business School professor speaking after Kodak's bankruptcy)

"Perfect products delivered past deadline kill companies faster than decent products delivered on time." Tim Ferriss (Author of The 4-Hour Workweek)

"Keep potential failures close to your core business – perhaps by introducing existing products into new markets or new products into familiar markets." Chris Zook (Consultant at Bain and Company)

"To manage failure, place 'little bets' and use rough and ready prototypes (where people are much more willing to give their honest opinions)." Peter Sims (Entrepreneur and author of Little Bets)

Section V: Marketing is Through the Customer's Eyes

80. The marketing is focused on the customers' wants and needs

"If there is any one secret of success, it lies in the ability to get the other person's point of view and see things from that person's angle as well as from your own." Henry Ford (Founder of Ford Motor Company)

"The sharpest entrepreneurs have a knack for viewing the world from the perspective of their customers." Martin Zwilling (Author of <u>Do You Have What It Takes to Be an Entrepreneur?</u>)

"A lot of marketing is listening to the customer and then repeating it back to them." Steve Harrison (Publicity and marketing expert)

"The aim of marketing is to know and understand the customer so well the product or service fits him and sells itself." Peter Drucker (Author and management theorist)

"Great marketing enters the conversation already going on in people's minds." Robert Collier (Self-help author in the early 20th century)

81. The marketing is targeted to one segment of the market

"It is said that if everyone is your customer, then no one is your customer." Tim Ferriss (Author of <u>The 4-Hour Workweek</u>)

"Market segmentation is the art of sacrifice." Seth Godin (American entrepreneur and author)

"Who you portray in your marketing is not necessarily the only demographic who buys your product. It is often the demographic that most people want to identify with or belong to." Tim Ferriss (Author of <u>The 4-Hour Workweek</u>)

82. The marketing and brand are memorable, simple and   targeted

The biggest challenge "was just getting people to pay attention. It's seventy percent of the battle." Dan Gilbert (Founder of Quicken Loans)

"Strong brands are clear about who they are and who they are not. They understand their unique promise of value." William Arruda (Personal branding expert)

"A strong brand promise makes it clear what to say NO to–saying yes to everything means you stand for nothing with high costs." Rick McPartlin (Consultant on revenue management)

"A brand for a company is like a reputation for a person. You earn reputation by trying to do hard things well." Jeff Bezos (Founder of Amazon)

83. The organization is aligned around the daily, consistent marketing effort

"Applying the marketing concept successfully requires support from the whole organization." Peter Drucker (Author and management theorist)

"The most effective advertising a company does is the way it conducts business." Alex Bogusky (Designer, marketer, author)

"People who work for you represent your brand. You want them to present themselves, and represent you, in a certain way. Whether employees realize it or not, everyone in a company interfaces with customers in one way or another, and their attitude will affect the brand. That's why we work so hard to make sure we have the right people representing our brand, and that everyone is in alignment once they get here." Marc Benioff (CEO of Salesforce.com)

"You are always on display. When it comes to your brand, there is no such thing as a transaction that doesn't count." David D'Alessandro (CEO of John Hancock)

Section VI: Sales Delivers Value to the Customer

84. Sales is recognized as essential

"Nothing happens until someone sells something." Thomas J. Watson (Founder of IBM)

"A company with plenty of sales can almost always fix its other problems. But a company without sales is close to dead." Seth Godin (American Entrepreneur and Author)

85. The sales team listens and focuses on solving the customer's problem

"Your salespeople talk too much." GE Customer Survey (from the mid-1990's)

"If you ask the right questions and then listen well, the customer will tell you exactly what their hot buttons are: those key problems that they need you to solve for them." David Shedd

"From a Harvard Business Review survey of customers; customers want to buy from people who understand their problems and understand what they are selling (their own companies' products)." Ken Morse (Serial entrepreneur, co-founder of 3Com)

"Stop selling what you have and start selling what they want." IBM sales training manual

"Sell the problem. No business buys a solution for a problem they don't have." Seth Godin (American entrepreneur and author)

"Ensure that the solution you are providing not only solves the customer's problems, but also that it matches the customer's expectations." David Shedd

"When the value is clear, the decision is easy." Steve Miller (Author, consultant, marketer)

86. The sales team is hard-working, persistent, and personable

"You can't win negotiated work sitting on your ass." Jack Baker (Founder of BMW Constructors)

"Do not take 'No' especially from a person who cannot say 'Yes'". Sales proverb

"All things being equal, people want to do business with their friends." Jeffrey Gitomer (Author of The Little Red Book of Selling)

87. The sales team is effective at building trust

"The reason that people don't believe you isn't that you're a liar. The reason we don't believe you is that the guy before you (and the woman before him) were unduly optimistic hypesters and we got burned. We believed, we leaned into it and we got stuck. If you catch yourself making a promise that's been made before, stop. Don't spend a lot of time and effort building credibility with this sort of promising, because it doesn't pay off. Make different promises, or even better, do, don't say." Seth Godin (American entrepreneur and author)

"Do what you say and when you say it. If you are going to be late or have made a mistake, notify the customer. This builds confidence which builds trust which builds lasting relationships. Lasting relationships are good for business and for you personally." Jack Baker (Founder of BMW Constructors)

88. Stories are integral to the sales process

"Humans are not ideally set up to understand logic; they are ideally set up to understand stories." Roger Schank (American cognitive psychologist)

"Selling is asking the right questions. Selling is listening. And selling is telling the right stories. Some stories are best told with pictures, some with numbers, some with analogies, some with comparisons, some with customer quotations, some with 3rd party data and some with internally observed metrics. You don't tell every story every time. But if you "frame and tame" - tell the right stories at the right time in the right way – you win more. And if you entire sales team is telling the right stories, you win a lot more." Paul McGhee (Sales trainer and sales consultant)

"Storytelling is by far the most underrated skill in business." Gary Vaynerchuk (Belarussian-American entrepreneur and author)

Chapter 7: Fundamentals of Personal Success

Section I: What is Success?

89. Understand your own definition of success

"What is success? To laugh often and much; To win the respect of intelligent people and the affection of children; To earn the appreciation of honest critics and endure the betrayal of false friends; To appreciate beauty; To find the best in others; To leave the world a bit better, whether by a healthy child, a garden patch or a redeemed social condition; To know even one life has breathed easier because you have lived; That is to have succeeded." Ralph Waldo Emerson (19th century American poet)

"Do your best. That is success." John Wooden (Famed UCLA basketball coach)

"There is a compelling lesson from Homer's *Odyssey*. At the end of a long life of suffering, maybe the best lesson that any of us can learn is to stay home, take care of our families, and be content with a life that brings simple happiness instead of glory." Rufus Fears (History professor at the University of Oklahoma)

"What man actually needs is not a tensionless state but rather the striving and struggling for a worthwhile goal, a freely chosen task." Viktor E. Frankl (Holocaust survivor, author of Man's Search for Meaning)

"Too many people spend money they haven't earned, to buy things they don't want, to impress people they don't like." Will Rogers (Early 20th century American cowboy, actor, humorist)

"When you are content to be simply yourself and don't compare or compete, everybody will respect you." Lao Tzu (Ancient Chinese philosopher)

"Be yourself. Everyone else is already taken." Oscar Wilde (Irish writer and poet)

90. Live life today… in the present time

"It is good to appreciate that life is now. Whatever it offers, little or much, life is now – this day – this hour." Charles Macomb Flandrau (American author)

"Most people spend the greatest part of their time working in order to live, and what little freedom remains so fills them with fear that they seek out any and every means to be rid of it." Johann Wolfgang von Goethe (From his novel The Sorrows of Young Werther published in 1774)

"There is nothing the busy man is less busied with than living; there is nothing harder to learn." Seneca (Ancient Roman stoic philosopher)

"I carry on as if I should never die. And I carry on as if I was going to die any minute." Zorba (Zestful Greek character from the novel Zorba the Greek)

"The art of life is to deal with problems as they arise, rather than destroy one's spirit by worrying about them too far in advance." Cicero (Roman orator, philosopher and statesman)

"Do not dwell in the past, do not dream of the future, concentrate the mind on the present moment." Buddha (Indian spiritual teacher and founder of Buddhism)

"Dost thou love life? Then do not squander time, for that is the stuff life is made of." Benjamin Franklin (A Founding Father of the United States)

"Time is the coin of your life. It is the only coin you have, and only you can determine how it will be spent. Be careful lest you let other people spend it for you." Carl Sandburg (Early 20th century American biographer and poet)

91. Be happy now

"Happiness is the one thing we seek for itself and not as a means to something else; whether we are aware of it or not, happiness is the true aim of all we do." Aristotle (Ancient Greek philosopher)

"The Great Western Disease lies in the phrase, I will be happy when... As in, I will be happy when I get that promotion, or I will be happy when I buy that house, or I will be happy when I get that money...[Looking back], many older people say they were so wrapped up in looking for what they didn't have that they seldom appreciated what they did have. They often wish they would have taken more time to enjoy it." Marshall Goldsmith (Leadership coach and author of What Got You Here Won't Get You There)

"Success is not the key to happiness. Happiness is the key to success. If you love what you are doing, you will be successful." Albert Schweitzer (Early 20th century German theologian, scientist and humanist)

"We can throw our whole lives away looking for things we already have but don't treasure." Peter Thomas (Canadian entrepreneur and author)

"The journey is better than the inn." Cervantes (Spanish author of Don Quixote)

Section II: Preconditions to Realizing Your Success

92. Take personal responsibility to realize your success

"Take 100% responsibility for your life." Jack Canfield (Co-author of Chicken Soup for the Soul)

"People are always blaming their circumstances for what they are. I don't believe in circumstances. The people who get on in the world are the people who get up and look for the circumstances they want and if they can't find them, make them." George Bernard Shaw (Irish playwright)

"Our remedies oft in ourselves do lie / which we ascribe to heaven." William Shakespeare (English playwright and author of All's Well that Ends Well)

"A man can fail many times, but he isn't a failure until he begins to blame somebody else." John Burroughs (American naturalist and essayist)

"There is only one element in life under our own control – our own excellence." Randy Komisar (American venture capitalist and author)

93. Set goals and create a plan to achieve them

"People with goals succeed because they know where they are going. It's as simple as that." Earl Nightingale (American motivational speaker and author)

"He who every morning plans the transaction of the day and follows out that plan, carries a thread that will guide him through the maze of the most busy life. But where no plan is laid, where the disposal of time is surrendered merely to the chance of incidence, chaos will soon reign."   Victor Hugo (19th century French dramatist, novelist, and poet)

"In training camps, therefore, we don't focus on the ultimate goal – getting to the Super Bowl. We establish a clear set of goals that are within immediate reach…When you set small, visible goals, and people achieve them, they start to get it into their heads that they can succeed. They break the habit of losing and begin to get into the habit of winning." Bill Parcells (Super Bowl-winning football coach)

"Throughout my athletics career, the overall goal was always to be a better athlete than I was at that moment…The improvement was the goal. The medal was simply the ultimate reward for achieving that goal." Sebastian Coe (Olympic Gold Medal winning runner)

"You've got to be careful if you don't know where you're going, because you might not get there."   Yogi Berra (Baseball Hall of Fame catcher)

94. Be positive, optimistic and enthusiastic

"Keep your thoughts positive because your thoughts become your words. Keep your words positive because your words become your actions. Keep your actions positive because your actions become your values. Keep your values positive because your values become your destiny." Peter Thomas (Canadian entrepreneur and author)

"Optimism is the faith that leads to achievement. Nothing can be done without hope and confidence." Helen Keller (Deaf and blind American author)

"I am fundamentally an optimist…Part of being optimistic is keeping one's head pointed toward the sun, one's feet moving forward." Nelson Mandela (First black President of South Africa)

"All is for the best in this best of all possible worlds." Dr. Pangloss (Character from Voltaire's novel Candide)

"Nothing great was every accomplished without enthusiasm." Ralph Waldo Emerson (19th century American poet)

"Enthusiasm is a vital element toward the individual success of every man or woman," Conrad Hilton (Founder of Hilton Hotels)

"Success is the ability to go from one failure to another with no loss of enthusiasm." Winston Churchill (British Prime Minister during World War II)

"A positive attitude may not solve all your problems, but it will annoy enough people to make it worth the effort."   Herm Albright (Writer, 1876-1944)

95. Forgive and avoid negativity

"Resentment is like drinking poison and then hoping it will kill your enemies." Nelson Mandela (First black President of South Africa)

"To be wronged is nothing unless you continue to remember it." Confucius (Ancient Chinese philosopher)

"I must forgive so that my desire for revenge does not corrode my being." Desmond Tutu (South African bishop and activist)

"Worrying gives a small thing a big shadow." Swedish proverb

"Any fool can criticize, condemn, and complain - and most fools do." Dale Carnegie (Author of How to Win Friends and Influence People)

Section III: 11 Behaviors of Successful People

96. Develop daily habits

"The individual who wants to reach the top in business must appreciate the might and force of habit. He must be quick to break those habits that can break him – and hasten to adopt those practices that will become the habits that help him achieve the success he desires."   J. Paul Getty (Founder of Getty Oil and the richest person in the world in the 1960's)

"We are what we repeatedly do. Excellence, then, is not an act, but a habit." Aristotle (Ancient Greek philosopher)

"A daily routine built on good habits is the difference that separates the most successful amongst us from everyone else." Darren Hardy (Publisher of Success magazine)

"We first make our habits and then our habits make us." John Dryden (17th century British poet)

97. Focus on the important, avoiding distractions

"The main thing is to keep the main thing the main thing." German proverb

"What you do is infinitely more important than how you do it. Doing something unimportant well does not make it important. Requiring a lot of time does not make a task important." Tim Ferriss (Author of The 4-Hour Workweek)

"The key is not to prioritize what's on your schedule, but to schedule your priorities." Stephen Covey (Author of The Seven Habits of Highly Effective People)

"It's only by saying 'no' that you can concentrate on the things that are really important." Steve Jobs (Founder and former CEO of Apple)

"Learning to ignore things is one of the great paths to inner peace." Robert J. Sawyer, (Canadian author of Calculating God)

"The successful warrior is the average man, with laser-like focus". Bruce Lee (Chinese-American actor and martial arts instructor)

"Switching from task to task causes us to forget what we were working on in the first place; in some cases, the forgetting rate can be as high as 40%. Workplace studies have found it takes up to 15 minutes for us to regain a deep state of concentration after a distraction such as a phone call." Joseph T. Hallinan (American journalist and author)

"Beware distractions; workers distracted by phone calls, E-Mails, and text messages suffer a greater loss of IQ than a person smoking marijuana." TNS Research (As quoted in Happier by Tal Ben-Shahar).

98. Keep things simple

"Simplicity, simplicity, simplicity! I say let your affairs be as two or three, and not a hundred or a thousand; instead of a million count half a dozen." Henry David Thoreau (19th century American poet and author of Walden)

"One does not accumulate but eliminate. It is not daily increase but daily decrease. The height of cultivation always runs to simplicity." Bruce Lee (Chinese-American actor and martial arts instructor)

"Besides the noble art of getting things done, there is the noble art of leaving things undone. The wisdom of life consists in the elimination of non-essentials." Lin Yutang (Chinese writer and inventor)
"The ability to simplify means to eliminate the unnecessary so that the necessary may speak." Hans Hofmann (German-Canadian paleontologist)

"Allah has removed from the Sahara all that is unnecessary so human beings can grasp the essence of things." Muslim proverb

99. Be effective at getting the right things done

"Do not mistake activity for achievement." John Wooden (Famed UCLA basketball coach)

"Get the important done first. What's been on your to-do list the longest? Start it first thing in the morning, don't check E-Mail and don't allow interruptions or lunch until you finish." Timothy Ferriss (Author of The 4-Hour Workweek)

"There is surely nothing quite so useless as doing with great efficiency what should not be done at all." Peter Drucker (Author and management theorist)

"Measuring busy-ness is far easier than measuring business. Busy-ness might feel good (like checking your email on Christmas weekend) but business means producing things of actual value. Often, the two are completely unrelated. What if you spent a day totally unbusy, and instead confronted the fear-filled tasks you've been putting off that will actually produce value once shipped?" Seth Godin (American entrepreneur and author)

100.   Do what you say

"Making noble resolutions is not as important as keeping the resolutions you have made already." Seneca (Ancient Roman Stoic philosopher)

"Well done is better than well said." Ben Franklin (A Founding Father of the United States)

"After all is said and done, more is said than done." Aesop (Greek writer credited with writing <u>Aesop's Fables</u>)

101.   Get going and move quickly

"The wise man does at once what the fool does finally." Niccolo Machiavelli (Renaissance Italian historian, philosopher, and author)

"Many a false step was made by standing still." Chinese proverb

"Putting off an easy thing makes it hard. Putting off a hard thing makes it impossible." George Claude Lorimer (19th century American pastor)

"The secret to getting ahead is getting started. The secret of getting started is breaking your complex, overwhelming tasks into small manageable tasks, and then starting on the first one." Mark Twain (19th century American author and humorist)

"The secret to success lies in careful preparation followed by speedy and decisive execution." Napoleon Bonaparte (Emperor of France from 1804 to 1815)

"Behave with urgency every day. Urgency is a set of thoughts and feelings as well as a compulsive determination to move and win now." Martin Zwilling (Author of <u>Do You Have What It Takes to Be an Entrepreneur?</u>)

"Perfection is the enemy of good. By this, I mean that a good plan executed with great vigor now is better than a perfect plan next week. Success is a very simple thing; and the determining characteristics are confidence, speed, and audacity – none of which can ever be perfect, but they can be good." George C. Patton (US General during World War II)

102.   Seize the opportunities that come your way

"To capitalize on luck, model Napoleon. Be quick, decisive and snatch at opportunities as they arise." Paul Johnson (Napoleon biographer)

"To every man there comes in his lifetime that special moment when he is figuratively tapped on the shoulder and offered a chance to do a very special thing, unique to him and fitted to his talents. What a tragedy if that moment finds him unprepared or unqualified for the work which would be his finest hour." Winston Churchill (British Prime Minister during World War II)

"The right man is the one who seizes the moment." Johann Wolfgang von Goethe (German writer, artist, and scientist)

"There are smart decisions and wise decisions. And one form of wisdom is the ability to judge when to let luck disrupt our plans. Not all time in life is equal. The question is, when the unequal moment comes, do we recognize it, or just let it slip? But, just as important, do we have the fanatic, obsessive discipline to keep marching, to push the opportunity to the extreme, to make the most of the chances we're given?" Jim Collins (Author of Good to Great and Great by Choice)

103. Be persistent

"Press on. Nothing in the world can take the place of persistence. Talent will not; nothing is more common than unsuccessful men with talent. Genius will not; unrewarded genius is almost a proverb. Education alone will not; the world is full of educated derelicts. Persistence and determination are omnipotent." Calvin Coolidge (30th President of the United States)

"In every field, grit (perseverance and passion for long-term goals) may be as essential as talent to high accomplishment." Angela L. Duckworth (Professor of psychology at the University of Pennsylvania)

"Persistence and consistent effort rule the day. We over-estimate what we can do in three months, but under-estimate what we can do in three years." David Shedd

"Patience and perseverance have a magical effect before which difficulties disappear and obstacles vanish." John Quincy Adams (6th President of the United States)

"If you are going to go through hell, keep going." Winston Churchill (British Prime Minister during World War II)

104. Be a person with integrity… be a good and kind person

"One person – a Raoul Wallenberg, an Albert Schweitzer, a Martin Luther King Jr. – one person of integrity can make a difference, a difference of life and death." Elie Wiesel (Author, Nobel Prize winner, Holocaust survivor)

"Professionalism is not just about appearance, ethics and a code of conduct. Professionalism is about having a lifetime dedication and commitment to higher standards and ideals, honorable values, and continuous self-improvement. Professionalism is a built in guidance system for always doing the best that you can do, always doing the right thing, and always standing tall for what you believe in." Jim Ball (Leadership consultant)

"Try not to become a man of success but rather to become a man of value." Albert Einstein (Nobel Prize winning physicist)

"Thousands of candles can be lit from a single candle, and the life of the candle, will not be shortened. Happiness never decreases by being shared." Buddha (Indian spiritual teacher and founder of Buddhism)

"It is rather embarrassing to have given one's life to pondering the human predicament and to find that in the end one has little more to say than: 'Try to be a little kinder.'" Aldous Huxley (English writer; author of Brave New World)

105. Rest, reflect, rejuvenate

"Make time off or 'Rejuvenation Time' one of your crucial, non-compromised, devoted productive priorities. Darren Hardy (Publisher of Success magazine) "The time to relax is when you don't have time for it." Sydney J. Harris (American journalist)

"We are a work-identified nation, that's the badge we wear - where we work, what we do - that's how we define ourselves. As such, we have a hard time giving ourselves permission to take vacation time." Katherine Crowley (American psychotherapist and small business consultant)

"Every now and then go away, have a little relaxation, for when you come back to your work your judgment will be surer. Go some distance away because then the work appears smaller and more of it can be taken in at a glance and a lack of harmony and proportion is more readily seen." Leonardo da Vinci (Italian Renaissance painter, sculptor, architect)

"Dolce Far Niente (The Sweetness of Doing Nothing)" Italian proverb

106.   Be good to yourself

"You can search throughout the entire universe for someone else who is more deserving of your love and compassion than you are yourself, and that person is not to be found anywhere. You yourself, as much as anybody, deserve your love and compassion." Buddha (Indian spiritual teacher and founder of Buddhism)

Chapter 8: Conclusion

Section I: Your Action is Required

107. The deepest insights, the most thought-provoking questions, the sagest wisdom down through the ages – all of these will do nothing to help move a company forward or make a person more successful. What is required is change and action.

"Perhaps the most valuable result of all education and learning is the ability to make yourself do the thing that you have to do, when it ought to be done, whether you like it or not; it is the first lesson that ought to be learned." Thomas Huxley (19th century English biologist)

"However many holy words you read, however many you speak, what good will they do you if you do not act upon them?" Buddha (Indian spiritual teacher and founder of Buddhism)

"Knowing is not enough; we must apply. Willing is not enough; we must do." Johann Wolfgang Von Goethe (German writer, artist, and scientist)

108. To move your company forward and to realize your personal success will require YOU to change

"It is always easier to talk about change than to make it." Alvin Toffler (American writer and futurist)

"I want to change. But, not if it is hard and not if it hurts." Anonymous Billions of Humans (but not You!!)

"Or have you only comfort, and the lust for comfort, that stealthy thing that enters the house a guest, and then becomes a host, and then a master." Kahil Gibran (Author of The Prophet)

"Life begins at the end of your comfort zone." Neale Donald Walsch (American author of <u>Conversations With God)</u>

"Everyone thinks of changing the world, but no one thinks of changing himself." Leo Tolstoy (Russian author of <u>War and Peace</u> and <u>Anna Karenina</u>)

Section II: Get Started Now

109. Start small

"A journey of a thousand miles must begin with the first step." Lao-Tzu (Ancient Chinese philosopher)

"Why is it that we often forget that big things are accomplished only by the perfection of little things?" John Wooden (Famed UCLA basketball coach)

"Success is the sum of small efforts, repeated day in and day out." Robert Collier (Self-help author in the early 20th century)

"We cannot do everything at once, but we can do something at once." - Calvin Coolidge (30th President of the United States)

110. But, get started today

"The difference between successful people and failures is not in the quality of their ideas or in the measure of their abilities, but in whether they trust their own judgment and dare to take action." Southern Chinese ethic (From Leslie T. Chang's <u>Factory Girls</u>)

"Though no one can go back and make a brand new start, anyone can start from now and make a brand new ending." Carl Bard (American writer and theologian)

"A year from now you may wish you had started today." Karen Lamb (American author)

"If we wait for the moment when everything, absolutely everything, is ready we shall never begin." Ivan Turgenev (19th century Russian writer)

"Tomorrow is always the busiest day." Spanish proverb

"How wonderful it is that nobody need wait a single moment before starting to improve the world." Anne Frank (Holocaust victim and author of <u>The Diary of a Young Girl</u>)

Chapter 9: About the Author

David M. Shedd is an experienced President / CEO level executive, an author, and an award winning speaker. David's passion and mission in all these activities is to help move companies forward and succeed through an unrelenting focus on the fundamentals.

As an executive, David has more than 11 years' experience as President of an up to $350M group of manufacturing, distribution and services companies. In this time, he has overseen a total of 20 different companies, including start-ups, business turn-arounds, and hyper-growth companies.

David holds a BA in Mathematics and an MBA degree with Distinction from the Wharton School of the University of Pennsylvania, where he graduated as a Palmer Scholar in the top 5% of the class. Prior to earning his MBA, David had broad international experience. He worked at the World Bank / International Finance Corporation, and he taught Mathematics and European History at an international high school near London, England.

David's first book, ***Build a Better B2B Business***, is available on Amazon.

David lives in Newport Beach, California with his wife and three children. He invites readers to visit his website at www.davidmshedd.com or www.110percentsuccess.com.

David's website is chock-full of information to help businesspeople move their companies forward. It contains:

- More than one hundred of his on-going blogs on business success and leadership.
- A bibliography (and book summaries) of excellent business, leadership and success books.
- Yet even more quotes on business and success.
- Referrals to other insightful business thought leaders.

Thank you for your interest. I wish you the best of luck in building, growing, and improving your company, moving it forward and propelling it and you to greater success!